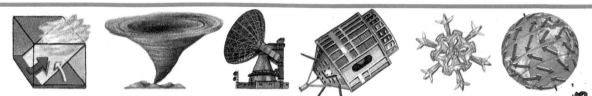

USBORNE UNDERSTANDING GEOGRAPHY
STORMS AND HURRICANES

Kathy Gemmel

Designed by **Andy Di**

Illustrated by
Gary Bines and Ian Jackson
Map illustration by **Janos Marffy**

Consultant
Francis Wilson

Series designer
Stephen Wright

Series editor
Jane Chisholm

SCHOLASTIC INC.

New York   Toronto   London   Auckland   Sydney

Contents

Weather satellites let us see what storms and hurricanes look like from space.

Some weather satellites circle the Earth 850km (530 miles) above the surface.

2

Weather and space

From space, the Earth looks like a beautiful blue and green marble, streaked with swirls of white cloud. The clouds, made up of tiny droplets of water or ice crystals, form huge spirals in places, like cream stirred into coffee. These are the Earth's storms and hurricanes.

Jupiter is a huge ball of gas, with no solid surface. It is over 1,300 times larger than the Earth and is thought to be extremely cold.

The Earth is the only planet in the Solar System with large amounts of water on it. Other planets have very different surfaces and weather conditions.

Mars is a red, dusty planet covered with craters and volcanoes. Strong winds blow the dust into the sky, making it look pinky orange.

On Venus, clouds move very, very fast and permanently hide the surface. Any rain that falls is acid.

78% nitrogen

21% oxygen

1% mixture of stable gases

The composition of the atmosphere near the ground

Water exists in varying amounts, either as invisible vapor (see page 6), tiny liquid droplets or solid ice crystals.

The Earth's atmosphere

Each of the nine planets which orbit the Sun is surrounded by a mixture of many different gases, called an atmosphere. The Earth's atmosphere is made up of several layers, about 900km (550 miles) deep. The force of gravity stops these layers from flying off into space.

The air in the lowest layer contains about 21% oxygen; most of the rest is nitrogen. As you climb through the atmosphere, the less oxygen there is. The air is said to become thinner and eventually fades away.

Any water present in the atmosphere is held in the lowest layer, called the troposphere. In some places this is about 8km (5 miles) thick, but in others it is up to 18km (12 miles) thick. Weather is the name given to whatever happens in the troposphere.

The troposphere is the layer of atmosphere nearest the Earth. It varies between 8km (5 miles) and 18km (12 miles) deep. All weather depends on the movement of air in the troposphere.

The stratosphere stretches to a height of 80km (50 miles). It contains the ozone layer. Ozone gas blocks many of the dangerous rays from the Sun.

The ionosphere is split into two: the mesosphere and the hot thermosphere. Both contain gases that absorb much of the Sun's harmful radiation.

The air in the exosphere is very thin. Its top is over 900km (550 miles) from the ground.

The magnetosphere marks the boundary between the Earth and space. It contains no gases.

3

Winds and pressure

Storms mean many things: huge black clouds rolling across the sky, thunder, lightning, torrents of lashing rain and sometimes hail or snow. But what really makes a good storm is wind.

Storm winds can cause enormous damage. They whip up the sea into colossal waves, which crash against coastal towns and cause flooding. They uproot trees, which fall and block roads. Some winds injure and even kill, as chunks of debris topple off buildings onto people below.

The most severe storms are those which begin above oceans in tropical and equatorial areas of the world.

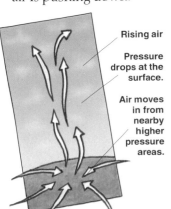

Survivors pick up the pieces after a storm in Bangladesh in 1991 killed thousands of people and left many more homeless. It was the worst storm in 20 years, with winds of over 200km/h (124mph).

How winds start

Amazingly enough, storm winds start off in exactly the same way as any breeze.

The weight of the atmosphere on the Earth's surface creates air pressure. Pressure varies from place to place, depending on what the air is doing at that point. Where air is sinking, there is high pressure near the ground, because more air is pushing down.

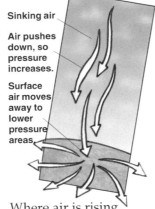

Sinking air

Air pushes down, so pressure increases.

Surface air moves away to lower pressure areas.

Where air is rising, less air pushes down, so there is low pressure near the surface.

Like air rushing out of a burst balloon, surface air is always on the move between high and low pressure areas, trying to even them out. This movement of air is what we call wind.

Rising air

Pressure drops at the surface.

Air moves in from nearby higher pressure areas.

Why air rises or sinks

As a general rule, warm air rises and cooler air sinks. This is because air expands (spreads) as it is warmed, which makes it lighter and want to rise. Cool air tends to sink as it is more dense (heavier).

All over the Earth, huge amounts of warm air rise due to the Earth's surface being heated by the Sun, more in some places than in others. The heat given back off by the Earth is what heats our atmosphere. As the heating is uneven, air pressure is constantly changing, which affects the way air moves (our wind).

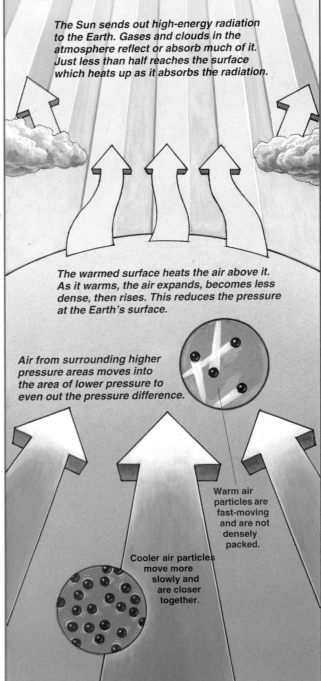

The Sun sends out high-energy radiation to the Earth. Gases and clouds in the atmosphere reflect or absorb much of it. Just less than half reaches the surface which heats up as it absorbs the radiation.

The warmed surface heats the air above it. As it warms, the air expands, becomes less dense, then rises. This reduces the pressure at the Earth's surface.

Air from surrounding higher pressure areas moves into the area of lower pressure to even out the pressure difference.

Warm air particles are fast-moving and are not densely packed.

Cooler air particles move more slowly and are closer together.

World heat and pressure differences

The Earth heats up more in some places than others because of the angle at which the Sun's rays strike the surface. Around the Equator, the Sun beats straight down, which means the heat there is intense. At the poles, the rays strike at much more of an angle. The heat is now spread over a wider area so it never gets very hot.

The uneven heating of the Earth produces a pattern of high and low pressure areas. Warm air rising at the Equator lessens the weight of air pushing down, which creates a band of low pressure. The opposite happens at the poles, where cold air sinks to form high pressure areas.

Temperatures remain high near the Equator all year, as the Sun is almost always directly overhead at noon each day.

Sun's rays

Two other bands of high and low pressure form as air circulates between the hot Equator and the freezing poles.

The rising equatorial warm air spreads out, cools and sinks down again around 30° north and south of the Equator, creating bands of high pressure there. This air then meets colder, denser air moving away from the poles and is forced to ride upward again, producing zones of low pressure around 60° north and south.

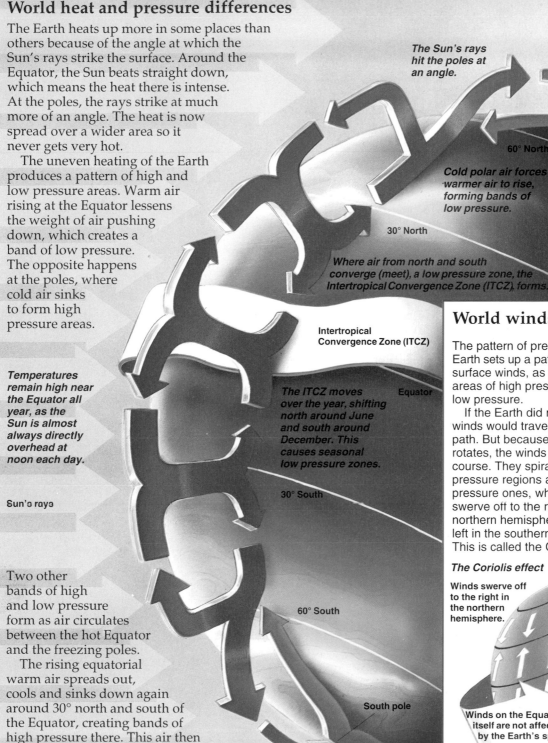

The Sun's rays hit the poles at an angle.

North Pole

60° North

Cold polar air forces warmer air to rise, forming bands of low pressure.

30° North

Where air from north and south converge (meet), a low pressure zone, the Intertropical Convergence Zone (ITCZ), forms.

Intertropical Convergence Zone (ITCZ)

Equator

The ITCZ moves over the year, shifting north around June and south around December. This causes seasonal low pressure zones.

30° South

60° South

South pole

World winds

The pattern of pressure over the Earth sets up a pattern of horizontal surface winds, as air travels from areas of high pressure to areas of low pressure.

If the Earth did not spin, these winds would travel in a straight path. But because the Earth rotates, the winds are pushed off course. They spiral out of high pressure regions and swirl into low pressure ones, which makes them swerve off to the right in the northern hemisphere and to the left in the southern hemisphere. This is called the Coriolis effect.

The Coriolis effect

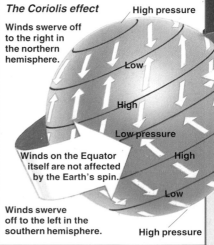

High pressure

Winds swerve off to the right in the northern hemisphere.

Low

High

Low pressure

High

Winds on the Equator itself are not affected by the Earth's spin.

Low

Winds swerve off to the left in the southern hemisphere.

High pressure

Moving air

Storms develop in different ways in different parts of the world. In areas between 30° and 60° north and south of the Equator, called midlatitude areas, storms are likely to happen when batches of air with different temperatures or humidities (levels of moisture) collide and battle for territory. In tropical areas, storms are like great wind machines, charged up by heat and moisture in the air.

The world's main winds are behind every storm, but the movement of air over local areas is what determines exactly where and how violent any one storm will be. The way the wind blows is affected by every mountain, body of water or wide plain.

Temperature and humidity

How warm, cool, wet or dry air is depends on the specific type of land - or sea - it passes over.

Rocks, sand, bare soil and forests absorb a lot of the Sun's rays. Currents of rising warm air, called thermals, rise from their heated surfaces.

Snow and ice reflect most of the Sun's rays, so the air temperature above the surface stays low.

When the Sun heats water, some of it turns into water vapor, which is so light it rises up through the air. This process is called evaporation.

Air that passes over warm water will be more humid (wetter) than air passing over land.

Air which has come a long way over dry land, such as a desert, will contain little water vapor.

A large quantity of air that has the same level of temperature and humidity is called an air mass. Warm air masses can hold more water than cold air masses. Air which comes from the warm seas of the tropics holds the most moisture and often produces the biggest storms.

Fronts

Storms in non-tropical areas happen mainly when air masses with different temperatures or humidities meet. The masses don't mix but remain separate, with a sloping boundary between them. This boundary is called a front.

Around 60°N and 60° S of the Equator, warm tropical air masses clash with cold polar air masses, creating a series of fronts, known as the polar front.

Depressions

Bulges occur along the polar front where one air mass pushes into the other. The temperature difference is greatest here, as warm air has pushed farthest into cold air (or vice versa). The warm air rises quickly, which reduces the weight of air pushing down. A region of low pressure, called a depression, develops.

Depressions usually mean unsettled, stormy weather, as air from all around swirls in to replace the rising air. This brings warm air into cold areas, creating what we call a warm front, and cold air into warm areas, producing a cold front.

The air rushing into a depression is our surface wind. Clouds form (see page 8) as the warm and cold air react.

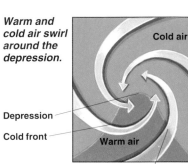

Polar front

60°N (latitude)

Depressions form at bulges along the polar front.

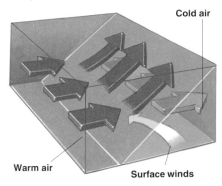

Warm and cold air swirl around the depression.

Cold air

Depression

Cold front

Warm air

Warm front

Where warm air pushes into colder, denser air, the warm air rides up over the cold. This is a warm front. Warm fronts often bring steady, prolonged rain, but not storms.

Cold air

Warm air

Surface winds

A cold front is where cold air cuts under warm air, forcing it to rise. Warm air rises more steeply and quickly at a cold front than at a warm front. This can produce heavy storm clouds (see page 8).

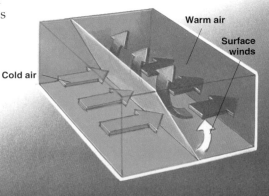

Warm air

Surface winds

Cold air

High-level winds

Where cold air meets warm air high above the Earth, they clash to produce very strong winds. These winds are called jet streams and they weave an uneven path around the Earth, west to east, about 10km (6 miles) above the Earth's surface. Jet streams occur at roughly the same latitude (60°N and S) as the polar front, but much higher.

As jet streams surge along, they disrupt air to either side of their paths, which affects the way air moves nearer the Earth. They drag highs and lows along, producing high pressure areas within bands of low pressure and vice versa.

The resulting surface air movements between highs and lows are our everyday winds, which change strength and direction constantly. The diagram below shows how jet streams work.

The jet stream thins out in places, which means air has to rise up from below to replace it. The low pressure this causes near the ground encourages depressions that are already developing.

Jet stream
thins out.

Air rises

Low pressure

Polar front

60° N

Surface winds

Pressure and strength

The closer together areas of high and low pressure are, the more they influence each other. When jet streams steer highs and lows close together, surface air has to move very fast to even out the pressure difference. If the pressure is very low, a lot of air has to swirl in to replace the rising air. Storm force winds are simply a combination of these two things: a lot of moving air, moving fast.

Winds strong enough to blow down whole trees occur when a lot of air rushes between high and low pressure areas.

Where the upper air squashes together, some is forced downward. This creates high pressure near the ground.

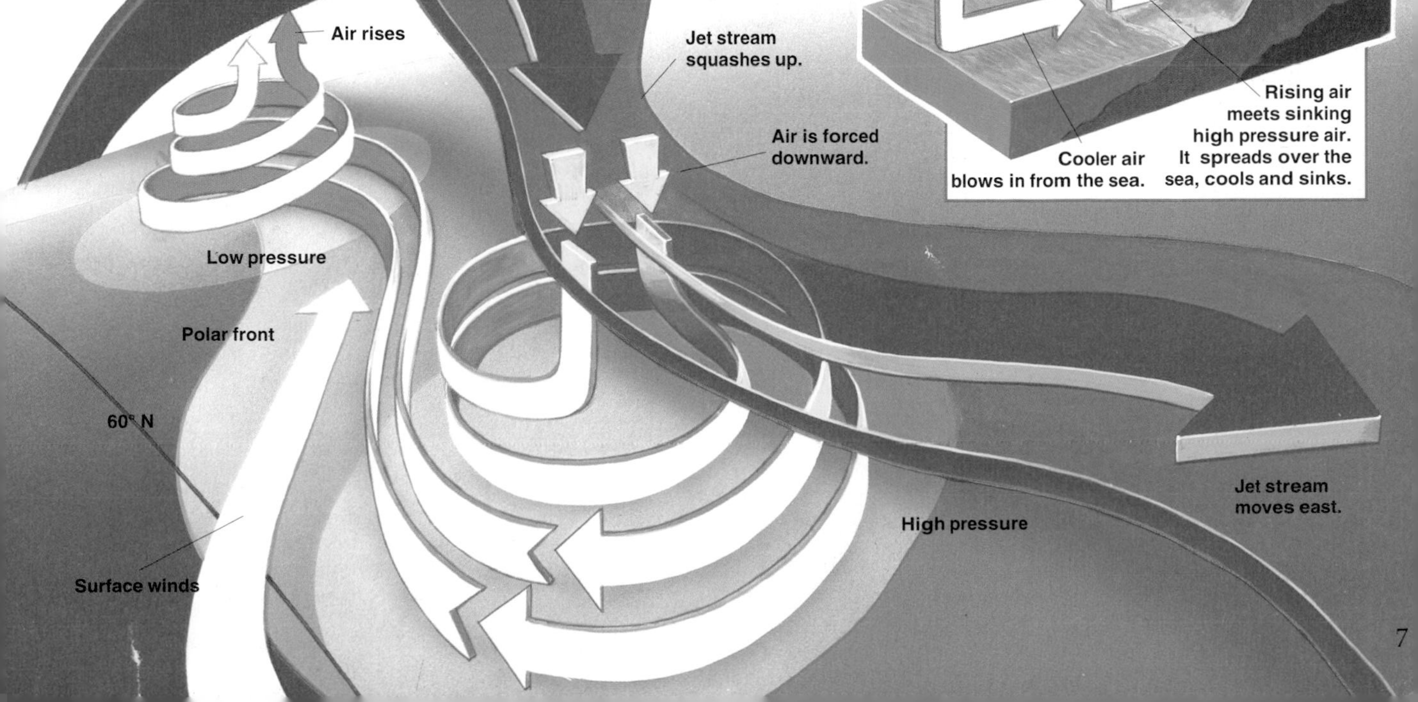

Jet stream
squashes up.

Air is forced
downward.

High pressure

Local winds

Certain areas have specific local wind patterns. When wind blows up a valley, it is said to funnel. The wind blows stronger, as the same amount of air tries to squeeze through a smaller gap.

The Mistral is a cold, dry wind that funnels violently down the Rhône river valley in France.

Wind funnel

Local sea breezes blow because land and sea heat up at different rates. Land heats quickly, as the Sun only has to heat the surface. At sea, waves carry heat down to the depths, so it takes longer to warm up.

Sea breezes form on days of high pressure, when land air warms quickly, rises and is replaced by cooler air moving in from the sea. Wet monsoons (see page 9) are large scale sea breezes.

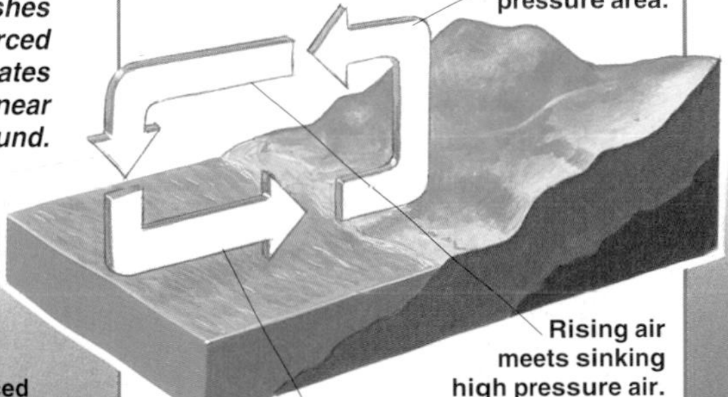

How a local sea breeze develops

Warm air rises leaving a local low pressure area.

Rising air meets sinking high pressure air. It spreads over the sea, cools and sinks.

Cooler air blows in from the sea.

Jet stream moves east.

Clouds, rain and more rain

Clouds are normally the first sign of an approaching storm, and with storm clouds comes rain. Although wind often causes more immediate damage, heavy rain can swell rivers until they burst their banks, flooding huge areas of land. As water surges along streets, it picks up mud, soil or waste debris and dumps it in places out of the main flow. This makes cleanup operations long and expensive.

Rainfall depends on moist air rising and cooling to a level which will let rainclouds form. The deeper the clouds, the more rain will fall.

Flooding can cause terrible damage to homes and businesses. This man's home is half underwater.

How clouds form

Clouds form when warm air rises, spreads, then cools as it gets higher. Any water vapor in the air condenses (turns back into a liquid) and forms tiny droplets around miniscule particles of dust in the air.

The droplets group together to form clouds. Air rises to form clouds in three main ways: by convection (heating from below), at hills, and at fronts.

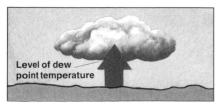

Level of dew point temperature

Convective clouds form as air heated by warm ground rises, cools and lets water vapor condense into droplets. The temperature at which this happens is called the dew point.

Hill clouds form when air cools as it is forced to rise over high ground.

Frontal clouds form when moist, warm air is forced to rise above denser cool air.

Different types of clouds form at different heights and temperatures. There can be many combinations in the sky at once. "Nimbus" is added to the name of a cloud that is likely to produce rain or snow.

Cumulonimbus (see box right) are the main storm clouds. They often form at cold fronts, where warm air is forced to rise quickly.

Cirrus clouds are high, feathery and made up of ice crystals which form as the water droplets freeze. Thickening of cirrus clouds show that a depression is approaching.

Cumulus clouds come at all heights and are fluffy, with flat bases. They usually mean fine, settled weather.

Stratus clouds form a low level layer. They often produce drizzle.

Rain

As water droplets move around the cloud, they collide with each other and eventually join to form larger droplets. Gradually these increase in size until they are too heavy for the air currents to keep them in the cloud and they fall as rain. This process is called coalescence.

Cumulonimbus clouds can swell to great heights with their tops up to 10km (6 miles) above the ground. The air is so cold at the top that the water droplets turn to ice.

The highest, thickest ones form in warm, moist air, where lots of air holding lots of water rises very quickly.

The rapidly-rising air means more of it condenses. This causes more droplets to collide, which produces lots of big, heavy drops of rain.

Did you know...

...that most rain in non-tropical areas starts off as snow? See page 12 for how snow is formed.

Rainy seasons

Certain tropical parts of the world, such as India and Southeast Asia, have regular periods when it rains a lot. These are called monsoons, from the Arabic word *mausim* which means "fixed season".

There are actually two monsoon seasons, a wet one and a dry one, caused by the reversal of wind direction at certain times of the year. The wet monsoon is the one most people mean when they talk about monsoons.

Wet monsoons

Wet monsoons are really just large scale sea breezes. By the end of May, the low pressure ITCZ is at its farthest north. This creates a big difference between very low pressure over northwestern India and high pressure over the Indian Ocean. The noonday Sun is directly overhead at this time, heating the land intensely. Vast amounts of air rise, which reduces the pressure even more.

Winds carrying lots of water vapor rush in from the Indian Ocean to replace the rising air. This wet air warms over the land and rises, forming great clouds. The moisture condenses to fall as heavy monsoon rain.

The fast-rising warm air causes local depressions which are pushed east by jet streams, spreading the rain to many regions. Millions of people rely on monsoon rain to water their crops. But sometimes there is too much rain and fields and homes are flooded and ruined.

Dry monsoons

In winter, the sun is no longer directly over the land and the ITCZ has moved south over the sea, causing low pressure there. Winds which are dry, due to moving a long way overland, blow in to replace the rising air over the low pressure Indian Ocean. This brings a dry season on land.

A homemade umbrella gives good protection from heavy monsoon rain.

Rice

India's wet monsoon

Low pressure ITCZ

The Himalaya Mountains block out northerly winds which would cool the intensely heated land.

N.W.India

Wet southwesterly winds blow over the land, causing heavy rain.

High pressure

Indian Ocean

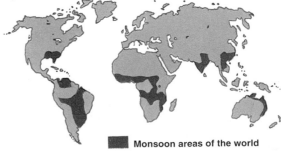

The wet monsoon blows from May to September in the northern hemisphere and December to February in the southern hemisphere.

■ Monsoon areas of the world

Thunderstorms

As you read this, about 2,000 thunderstorms are exploding all over the world. There are more thunderstorms than any other type of storm, with some tropical countries, such as Nigeria, having one roughly every two days.

Wherever there is thunder, there is lightning too. Bad thunderstorms in Florida, USA, in March 1993, brought an amazing 5,000 lightning strikes per hour. Carrying huge amounts of electrical energy, lightning is the most dangerous part of a thunderstorm.

Many people are killed by lightning every year. As well as destroying lives, it can start forest fires, ruin crops and set homes on fire. Computers and other electrical machines are at risk from power surges if lightning strikes.

Thunderclouds

Lightning and thunder come from huge cumulonimbus clouds. These are at their biggest at cold fronts, or when moist tropical air hits warm air rising over hot land. The cloud billows upward right through the troposphere and spreads below the stratosphere.

Tiny ice crystals at the top of the cloud spread into a shape like a blacksmith's anvil. The anvil is called a thunderhead.

The tops of thunderclouds are lit by the Sun, so they look orangey-yellow or white.

Some cumulonimbus are so thick they block out the sunlight, making it dark in daytime.

Lightning

Inside the cloud, water droplets and ice crystals are pushed around by air currents, making them bump and rub together. This movement, called friction, charges them with static electricity. Positively charged droplets and crystals gather at the top of the cloud and a negative charge builds up at the base.

Eventually the electrical energy difference between the top and bottom (about 100 million volts) becomes too great for the cloud. To equalize the difference, a giant spark leaps toward an oppositely-charged point on the ground.

Static electricity builds up in the cloud. Positive charges gather at the top and negative charges at the base.

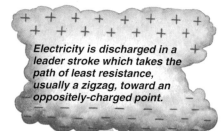

Electricity is discharged in a leader stroke which takes the path of least resistance, usually a zigzag, toward an oppositely-charged point.

A charged stroke from the ground leaps up to meet the leader and shoots back up to the cloud. This return stroke is the one we see as lightning.

One flash can be made of up to 40 strokes. They travel so fast, all you see is a flicker.

Thunder

The air inside the return lightning stroke is over five times hotter than the surface of the Sun (over 33,000°C, 86,000°F). In this heat, the air expands (spreads) rapidly, creating shockwaves in the air to either side. These waves make the noise we know as thunder.

If a storm is directly overhead, you hear a sharp crack of thunder at the same time as seeing the lightning. Otherwise, you hear the thunder shortly after the lightning because light travels faster than sound. Both thunder and lightning stop when the charges in the cloud have been evened out.

Did you know...

...that to find out how far away a storm is, you just need to count the seconds between the lightning and the thunder? Divide by 3 for the distance in km and 5 for miles.

Exciting lightning

Lightning appears in more forms than a fork flashing from the sky. Some of the odder ones have baffled scientists for years.

Sheet lightning happens when the charges are equalized inside or between clouds. The fork is shielded from the ground by a sheet of cloud, so all we see is a flash of light.

Saint Elmo's Fire is a curious gleam, sometimes seen over masts or other high points when a storm cloud is above. It is thought to occur when electricity around the cloud is very strong.

Many claim to have seen a floating ball of orange light, about the size of a tennis ball, lasting for several minutes. Nobody is sure how or where this ball lightning is formed.

Microbursts

Air rising quickly creates powerful updrafts in a thundercloud, but there are also strong downdrafts of air, called microbursts, that produce columns of heavy rain.

When a microburst hits the ground, it smashes outward, creating winds of up to 160km/h (100mph). This is very dangerous for aircraft. In 1982, 153 people were killed in New Orleans when their plane was caught in a microburst just after taking off.

Heavy rain

Strong horizontal winds

Aircraft usually fly above the level of thunderclouds to avoid microbursts.

Where lightning strikes

Lightning takes the fastest route to the ground. As air does not conduct (carry) electricity well, each stroke picks a high point to carry its charge. Single trees and steeples are prime targets.

Weather experts use radar (see page 18) to warn aircraft where they may come across dangerous lightning.

(see page 18)

A church protected by a lightning rod on the spire

Copper strip

Metal plate

Tall buildings often have lightning rods on the roof. These conduct the charge down copper strips to a metal plate on the ground. The ground absorbs the charge and the lightning is kept safely on the outside of the building. This is called earthing.

Keep away from lone trees in a storm, as bark has been known to explode off them as the sap (a good conductor) expands in the heat of a strike. Water is a good conductor, so keep away from lakes, too.

A safe place to be is in a car. The metal body acts as a protective cage, letting the charge run over it, then harmlessly into the ground through the wet wheels. Aircraft have special conductors that prevent any one spot from receiving the full force of a strike.

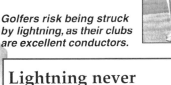

Golfers risk being struck by lightning, as their clubs are excellent conductors.

Lightning never strikes twice?

This is nonsense. An unlucky park ranger in Virginia, USA, was struck seven times between 1942 and 1977.

The Campanile of San Marco, by far the tallest building in Venice, has been struck by lightning many times.

Wet storms and dry storms

Storm winds often bring a lot more than rain. They can bring snow, hail and even dust or sand. Severe snowstorms cut off whole communities for days, stranding people and animals. Equally widespread dust storms cause long-lasting chaos and destruction.

Hail is very common during thunderstorms. All over the world, heavy hailstorms cause expensive damage to crops each year.

How snow is formed

Snow is formed in clouds which stretch up into freezing air. These clouds are a mixture of ice crystals, water droplets, and supercooled water droplets (droplets which can exist as water below freezing). The supercooled droplets freeze instantly when they touch ice crystals, which then grow and stick to other ice crystals, forming snowflakes. Snowflakes fall when they become too heavy to be held up by air currents in the cloud.

Supercooled droplet

Ice crystal

A snowflake's shape depends on the height and temperature at which it is formed.

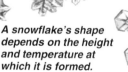

Because warmer air holds more moisture than cold, the heaviest snow falls around freezing point, not when it is very cold.

If the temperature is above freezing near the ground, the snowflakes melt and land as rain.

Snowstorms

When a snowstorm's winds reach 62km/h (39mph), it is called a blizzard. Blizzards often happen far inland in big continents, like North America, where temperatures in winter are very low. Their strong winds whip up powdery, dry snow from the ground and blow it along with already heavily falling snow.

High winds pile snow up into great drifts against buildings and on roads, causing massive disruption.

Blizzards often cause whiteouts, where the ground and sky blend into one other. Animals, blinded by snow, walk with their backs to the wind until they come to a fence, where they either starve or freeze to death. In mountains, the poor visibility and high winds can cause skiers and climbers to get lost or badly injured.

Ice storms

Supercooled droplets can fall without forming snowflakes, freezing instantly on contact with cold surfaces. The weight of ice that builds up can bring down telegraph poles and even capsize ships as they become top-heavy. Aircraft flying through freezing clouds risk losing control as droplets freeze onto the engine.

Hailstorms

Hail starts off as ice crystals in big cumulonimbus thunderclouds. As strong updrafts push the crystals around the cloud, they collide with supercooled droplets, which freeze around them to form tiny hailstones. More layers of ice coat the hailstones as they are swept around the cloud. Finally the stones are so big, they fall to Earth.

How hailstones are formed

Path of hailstone

Strong air currents

Ice crystal collides with droplet, which freezes around it.

Hailstone is carried around the cloud and coated with more ice.

Heavy hailstone falls.

Snowflakes may form, but the air is moving so fast that hail is more likely.

Hail can kill. Most hailstones that reach the ground weigh less than 1 gram (0.035oz), but occasionally much larger ones fall. In 1986, a storm of hailstones each weighing over 1kg (2.2lbs) killed 92 people in Bangladesh.

A giant hailstone sliced open

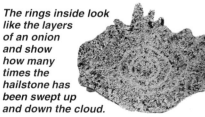

The rings inside look like the layers of an onion and show how many times the hailstone has been swept up and down the cloud.

Hail mystery

Although hail falls in storms, single blocks of ice have been known to fall from a clear sky. One fell in Spain in 1929, weighing nearly 2kg (4.5lb). Nobody knows where it came from.

Dust storms

Dust storms are very strong winds that lift huge quantities of dust, often to great heights, then drop it down again. The winds are created at fronts where warm air rises quickly. Spectacular, dust-laden clouds form as the rising air condenses, but as there is very little water vapor in the dry, desert air, no rain falls.

Giant bands of dust 2,400km (1,500 miles) long and 640km (400 miles) wide, called *haboobs*, are blown across the African deserts along the line of a front. In the Sudan there are about 24 *haboobs* a year.

Sand storms

Sand particles are larger and heavier than dust particles, so the sand tends to be blown along nearer the ground. Over 4m (13ft) can pile up against homes and fences, causing similar problems to snowstorms, as drifts disrupt travel and cut off villages. People and animals risk suffocation in severe sand storms.

Sand storms erode (blow away) vital soil from crop-growing areas, turning them into deserts where nothing can grow. Erosion causes great famine in areas of Africa, central Asia and South America.

Delicate machinery can be ruined, either by dust getting into the workings, or by the force of the sand or dust blasting against it.

Red snowstorm

The dry, warm wind of the Sahara desert, the *Sirocco,* sweeps up dust and sand which is then blown vast distances by high level winds. Tiny particles of red Sahara dust in the air have caused red snow to fall over the Alps. Red rain has fallen as far north as the United Kingdom.

Red rain

Red snow

Red Sahara dust is lifted by the Sirocco, then carried up into northern Europe by high level air waves.

Drifts of sand

This man wears a scarf over his mouth and nose to stop the sand from suffocating him.

13

Whirlwinds

There are several different kinds of whirlwinds, but the fiercest is the tornado, whose winds are the most powerful on the planet.

Stretching down from heavy thunderclouds and accompanied by lightning, rain and hail, tornadoes are a terrifying sight. Along with their watery cousins, waterspouts, tornadoes cause great damage to anything in their path.

Gentle whirlwinds, called devils, occur in good weather and are especially common in hot, dry areas.

How tornadoes start

Tornadoes form in thunderclouds, where strong updrafts of air come close to an unusually strong downdraft. This tends to happen most during violent storms, often at cold fronts, where warm air is forced to rise quickly. The word itself, tornado, comes from the Spanish for thunderstorm, *tronada*.

The strong updrafts leave a low pressure area in the cloud. Air rushes in to replace the updrafts and even out the pressure. Because the updrafts are so strong, the incoming air is all warmer air from below, which strengthens the updrafts even more. As it streams in and up, this air twists the already soaring air into a spinning spiral.

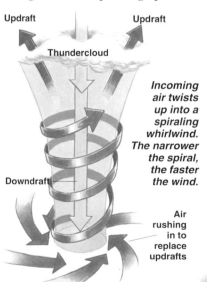

Updraft   Updraft

Thundercloud

Incoming air twists up into a spiraling whirlwind. The narrower the spiral, the faster the wind.

Downdraft

Air rushing in to replace updrafts

A tornado's "trunk"

As warm air is drawn upward into the base of the thundercloud, it cools and condenses into tiny cloud droplets. The strong downdraft pushes the droplets below the base of the thundercloud into a hanging bump of white cloud. This is the first visible sign of a tornado.

As more and more air is sucked up, it condenses at lower and lower levels, until it forms a great funnel of cloud. By the time it reaches the ground, the funnel looks like a huge elephant's trunk dipping down from the thundercloud.

Tornado touchdown

The "trunk" makes a hissing sound as it swings down, which turns into a roar as it touches the ground. Its appearance darkens dramatically as dust and debris are sucked up into the funnel.

Any loose object is in danger of disappearing up into the whirling dust. Animals, people and even trucks can be plucked from the ground, carried some distance, then dropped. The funnel of the tornado hops from place to place, which means one house can be destroyed and the next untouched.

The pressure inside a tornado can be as low as half the usual pressure of the atmosphere (see page 20). This can cause explosions, as higher pressure air inside buildings bursts out. Doors and windows should be opened as a tornado approaches, so that air can escape gradually and cause less damage.

Objects as big as cars can be picked up and smashed like toys.

Loose objects become deadly missiles as they are hurled through the air.

Freak showers

Frogs, fish and even cats and dogs can be sucked off the ground by a tornado and then spat out as it weakens, showering down like rain.

An intense storm in the Australian outback in 1994 showered down hundreds of freshwater fish, while in England in 1978, geese rained down in a line 45km (28 miles) long. Tornadoes were blamed for both.

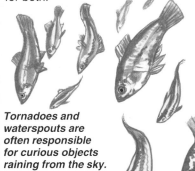

Tornadoes and waterspouts are often responsible for curious objects raining from the sky.

Tornadoes are often called twisters, because they can twist the tops off trees.

Where tornadoes go

Tornadoes move forward with the storm at around 56km/h (35mph), with spinning winds of up to 480km/h (300mph). The funnel can be very narrow, or up to 500m (1,625ft) wide. As many as forty separate funnels can form, as one storm sweeps across the land. The roar of a raging tornado can be heard 40km (25 miles) away.

Most tornadoes last no longer than half an hour and some only a few minutes. They weaken when the air sucked in is no longer warm enough to fuel the updrafts. As the updrafts lessen, the pressure evens out and the winds drop.

Tornado Alley

The stretch of plains land between Texas and Illinois in the USA is known as Tornado Alley, because of the frequency of tornadoes.

The worst recorded was on March 18, 1925. During its 3½ hour spree, it killed 689 people, injured 1,980, destroyed 4 towns, damaged 6 others and left 11,000 people homeless.

The yellow arrow shows Tornado Alley. 300 tornadoes were recorded in this area alone in June 1990.

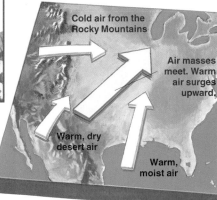

Cold air from the Rocky Mountains

Air masses meet. Warm air surges upward.

Warm, dry desert air

Warm, moist air

Waterspouts

Waterspouts are simply tornadoes over water. The funnel is mainly made up of condensed air droplets, but it sucks up water as it touches the sea, sending out whirling spray from its base. The largest, a huge 1½ km (1 mile) high, was recorded off the coast of Australia in 1898. Waterspouts can pick up crabs or shells which rain down as they hit land. As they weaken, all the water crashes down, wrecking boats or coastal buildings.

In the past, waterspouts were mistaken for sea monsters.

Fire devils

When a large fire heats the air above it, strong thermals can develop. These suck in air from all around, which rushes in and up, drawing the fire up into a spinning pillar.

The incoming air provides more oxygen for the fire, making it burn even more fiercely. Nothing can survive a fire devil, or even get near enough to put it out.

Fire devils spin across the ground at great speed.

Dust and wind devils

Unlike tornadoes, dust devils can occur with no clouds in the sky. Most common on hot, dry days in the desert, they start as narrow thermals, which are spun into mini whirlwinds as air rushes in from all directions. Dust devils pick up dust or sand as they spin and can rise as high as 1km (½ mile).

Wind devils are just dust devils without the dust. They whip leaves from trees and leave flattened patches in fields.

Ancient desert tribes thought dust devils were spirits, called "ginni". This is where the genie of the Arabian Nights comes from.

Hurricanes

The hurricane, with its furious winds, banks of cloud and torrential rains, is the most spectacular single feature of the Earth's great weather machine.

About 2,000 times wider than tornadoes, hurricanes sweep away everything in their paths and run up damage bills which can cripple the economies of whole countries. They often take many lives. Where tornadoes are brief and relatively confined, hurricanes are huge, slow-moving and unstoppable.

The word hurricane comes from the West Indian word for "big wind", *urican*, and is only one name for what weather experts call a tropical cyclone. In the Pacific, they are called typhoons; in the Bay of Bengal, cyclones; and in Australia, willy-willies.

Inside the storm

As wet air spirals up the central column of the storm, it cools and the water vapor condenses to form walls of huge cumulonimbus clouds. Called rainbands, these walls produce very heavy rain and hail.

Down the middle of the column is the eye of the hurricane, where air is slowly sinking. It varies from 6km (4 miles) to a huge 60km (37 miles) wide. The smaller the eye, the faster winds swirl around it.

Inside the eye, it is calm, with high temperatures and clear skies. As the eye passes, the fierce wind and heavy rain stop, only to start again, from the opposite direction, as the other side of the hurricane arrives.

Where they start

Although the exact conditions needed for hurricanes to form are unknown, there are two essential ingredients: warmth and moisture. Hurricanes only develop at sea, and only in warm water, of 27°C (80°F) or over. This is why they happen mainly in tropical regions, within 1,600km (1,000 miles) of the Equator (20°N and S).

There are many stormy low pressure systems over the tropical oceans, but for a tropical storm to become a hurricane, its winds must reach a speed of 117km/h (73mph). This often happens with depressions that form over Africa then travel out over the Atlantic, drawing up warm, wet ocean air as they go.

Winds deflected by the Coriolis effect swirl around the deepening depression, twisting the rising air into a whirling cylinder. Hurricanes never form on the Equator itself because the winds there are not deflected enough by the Coriolis effect.

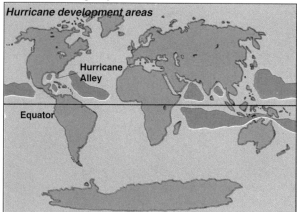

Hurricane development areas

Hurricane Alley

Equator

Peak hurricane time is early autumn in the western Atlantic, Pacific and Indian oceans, where the low pressure ITCZ encourages developing depressions. January is peak time in the southern hemisphere.

Hurricanes happen about three times more often in the Pacific than the Atlantic, which makes areas in the southeast of Asia the most frequently hit.

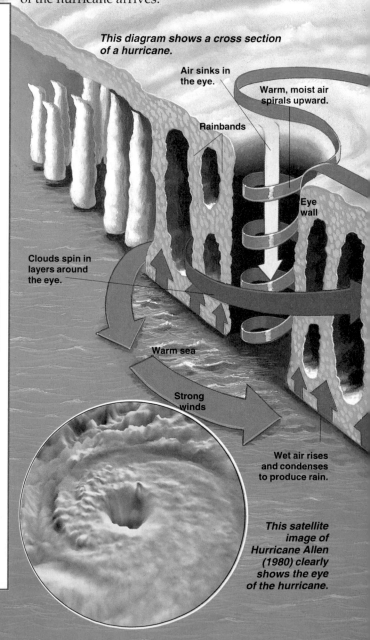

This diagram shows a cross section of a hurricane.

Air sinks in the eye.

Warm, moist air spirals upward.

Rainbands

Eye wall

Clouds spin in layers around the eye.

Warm sea

Strong winds

Wet air rises and condenses to produce rain.

This satellite image of Hurricane Allen (1980) clearly shows the eye of the hurricane.

How they keep going

A moderately-sized hurricane produces more energy than a nuclear explosion. This, per day, is about 1,000 times more than all the electrical power generated in the whole of the USA.

The key to a hurricane's energy is water vapor. As water vapor condenses, it gives off a lot of heat energy. In a hurricane, enormous amounts of heat are released because all the air coming in is warm and moist. This heat energy fuels the brewing hurricane, making it grow in size and strength.

The average hurricane is 480km (300 miles) wide and lasts around 10 days. Its winds can gust up to 240km/h (150mph), which is fast enough to drive a plank right through the trunk of a palm tree. Winds of this violence whip up waves which swell to 20m (66ft) high. These will easily capsize yachts, and toss around even the biggest ship.

Icy cirrus clouds are thrown outward by the spin.

Boats caught in severe hurricanes rarely survive the combined battering of wind, waves, rain and hail.

Direction of hurricane movement

Where they stop

Hurricanes follow warm sea currents west, helped along by cloud-level easterly winds. Sometimes they change direction abruptly, swerved by local winds or, more often, by changes in the warm current. This makes their paths difficult to predict.

When the air coming in from below is no longer moist and warm, hurricanes start to break up. This usually happens when they move inland, or over cooler water. Clouds gradually fill in the eye and the hurricane weakens and eventually dies.

Hurricane force winds do occasionally survive to hit areas outside the tropics, but without the warm sinking air in the eye, these storms are not officially classed as hurricanes.

Naming hurricanes

Most hurricane areas have local lists of hurricane names. The first each year begins with A, the second with B and so on. As soon as a storm's winds reach 117km/h (73mph), it is given the next name on the list.

This system was started in 1890 by Clement Wragge, an Australian weatherman, who named hurricanes after politicians he disliked. When they protested, women's names were used instead. This system remained until 1975, but now every second hurricane has a man's name.

Hurricane Andrew, in 1992, was the USA's most costly natural disaster.

Storm watching from above

A tiny change in the path of a storm or hurricane can mean the difference between life and death: whether it flattens a town, or blows itself out over unpopulated land. It is very important to know how fast a storm is developing, so that areas in danger can be evacuated.

Enormous size and slow movement make it easier to predict the progress of a hurricane than a tornado, but never certain. The ocean is so vast that even a storm as big as a hurricane can be hard to spot.

Weather experts use a variety of methods to forecast and track the paths of big storms. A lot of vital information now comes from way above the storm, from aircraft and spacecraft.

Weather satellites

The first weather satellite, Tiros 1, was launched into space in 1960. For the first time, weather experts were able to study remote areas of the oceans, where hurricanes could be forming. Ten days after launch, Tiros 1 spotted a developing hurricane approaching Brisbane, in Australia. The early warning gave people time to prepare, saving many lives.

Today, there are two types of weather satellite: polar-orbiting and geostationary. Between them, they transmit cloud pictures which cover the whole surface of the Earth.

Geostationary satellite, Meteosat 1

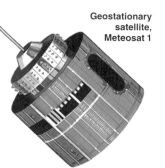

Geostationary satellites hover 36,000km (22,370 miles) above the Equator. They take the same time to orbit the Earth (24 hours) as the Earth takes to spin around its axis. So they always monitor the weather above the same spot.

Polar-orbiting satellite, ERS-1

Polar-orbiting satellites go over both poles, 850km (530 miles) high. One orbit takes 100 minutes, by which time the Earth has rotated 25°. This means a new strip of the Earth's surface is monitored each orbit.

Satellite images

The satellite images you see on television forecasts are produced using instruments called radiometers. These record the strength of reflected light and heat. They send the information to processing stations on the ground where it is turned into images.

Infrared cameras take cloud pictures 24 hours a day, by recording the amount of heat given off by different surfaces. The coldest surfaces, such as the freezing tops of thunderclouds, show up white, and the warmest show up black. Storms and hurricanes are identified by a circular swirl of cloud.

Successive images from geostationary satellites can be joined up to produce "movies" that show the continuous movement of clouds over one spot. Polar-orbiting images are sharper because they are closer to the Earth, but cannot be joined up so easily.

Infrared image of Hurricane Gilbert, September 14, 1988.

Infrared image of Hurricane Gilbert, September 15, 1988.

By measuring how far clouds move between images, experts can work out the speed and direction of the upper winds of a hurricane.

In daytime, the amount of sunlight reflected from different surfaces is recorded. This produces visible images of storm clouds and the land beneath.

The surface of the sea below the swirling clouds can be seen very clearly in this visible satellite image of a hurricane.

Weather planes

Weather planes, like the one below, take temperature and pressure readings and report on cloud forms and wind strength, to let experts know where to expect bad storms. Specially equipped "hurricane hunters" record conditions around, and even inside, large storms and hurricanes (see right and page 24).

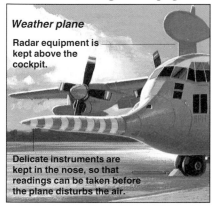

Weather plane

Radar equipment is kept above the cockpit.

Delicate instruments are kept in the nose, so that readings can be taken before the plane disturbs the air.

Radar scanning

Since World War II, radar has been used to track storms spotted by satellite, and warn ships and aircraft to stay clear. The equipment is usually on the ground, but is also used on aircraft or ships.

Radars show bands of rain. They bounce waves of radiation off raindrops and reflect them back to receiving dishes. From there, they are processed into images.

Radar is at its most useful for hurricanes within 240km (150 miles) of land. It picks up the spiral bands of rain around the eye, telling experts about the strength of the storm.

A radar called Doppler radar, can spot tornado-producing clouds 20 minutes before the funnel reaches the ground.

Taming hurricanes

Little can be done to halt a hurricane, but attempts have been made to reduce its power by artificially making the eye wider. The bigger the eye, the slower winds blow around it. In theory, this means the hurricane will do less damage. This is called seeding.

A hurricane hunter scatters chemicals outside the cloud wall around the eye. These make ice crystals in the cloud grow until they are heavy enough to fall through it. As they fall, the crystals melt into heavy rain, releasing a lot of heat energy. The heat disrupts the wall of the eye, which re-forms farther out, creating a larger eye with weaker winds.

Cloud seeding of Hurricane Debbie in 1969 is thought to have slowed winds by almost a third. Planes flew into the eye wall five times in two eight-hour periods.

Hurricane hunter

Cloud seeding does not always work, and there is a danger that the heat energy from the rainmaking process can simply fuel the hurricane without enlarging the eye. This makes it a risky experiment to try too near land.

Seeding has also been used to reduce large hailstones.

The chemicals provide more particles for hailstones to form around, making each one smaller and less damaging. Ideally, these smaller hailstones then melt and fall as rain.

Rainmaking can bring rain to drought-ridden areas, but it is very unreliable. It is impossible to tell how much rain would have fallen from the cloud anyway.

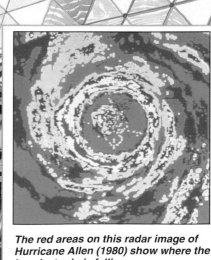

The red areas on this radar image of Hurricane Allen (1980) show where the heaviest rain is falling.

Storm watching from below

Storm watching from the sky and from space gives a good idea of what dangerous storm systems will do. But there are other, ground-based ways to predict and chart storms. An essential tool for a storm watcher is a weather map. The ones you see on television weather reports are largely made up from observations from ground weather stations.

Weather stations

Regular measurements of rainfall, pressure and wind speed are made at exactly the same time at over 51,000 weather stations all around the world. Every station uses the same system of measurement, whether it is on a ship at sea, or computer operated in a remote area, such as one of the polar regions. Some weather stations specialize in storm watching.

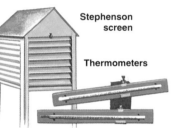

Stephenson screen

Thermometers

Thermometers measure temperature. They are kept inside a slatted box, called a Stephenson screen, which keeps out direct sunlight, but lets air flow freely. Temperature is measured in °Celsius or °Fahrenheit.

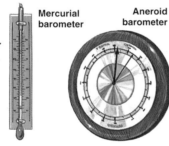

Mercurial barometer

Aneroid barometer

Barometers measure air pressure, in millibars (mb), or pounds per square inch (psi). The average pressure of the atmosphere is 1013mb (29.91psi). This can fall to 910mb (26.87psi) in the low pressure eye of a hurricane.

Anemometer

Wind vane

Anemometers measure wind speed. The stronger the wind, the faster the cups spin. The wind's direction, measured using a wind vane, is always stated as where it comes from, not where it is going.

Hygrometers measure humidity (moisture in the air). Humidity is measured as a percentage of the maximum amount of water vapor the air can hold at a certain temperature.

Specialized stations use Doppler radar to detect weather likely to spawn tornadoes, then put out tornado watches to warn the public. Some people spend their spare time chasing tornado-producing clouds, in the hope of filming or photographing one.

Maps and forecasts

Readings from all over the world are fed into powerful computers, which analyze and code the information. It is then sent electronically to central forecasting stations, where it is decoded and plotted onto weather maps. These are updated every hour.

Weather maps are really pressure charts. Lines called isobars join up points with the same atmospheric pressure, usually at ground level. The closer the isobars, the steeper the change in pressure and the stronger the wind. The position of highs and lows, fronts, frontal depressions and tropical cyclones (hurricanes) can all be worked out from the isobars.

Warm fronts often bring wide-spread rain, followed by clouds.

Cold fronts often bring narrow belts of rain and thunderstorms.

When a cold front catches up to a warm front, it undercuts and forces up the warm air, often producing heavy rainclouds. This is called an occluded front.

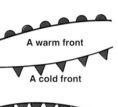

A warm front

A cold front

An occluded front

A storm on a weather map

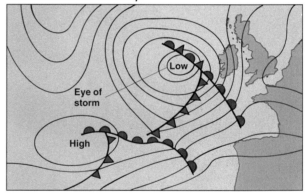

Low

Eye of storm

High

Information from weather maps is fed into an extremely powerful computer, which spots trends and calculates what the new measurements will be according to its own computer model of the atmosphere.

By doing this repeatedly and very quickly, forecasts can be made up to six days in advance. Forecasters use maps produced by the computer, as well as the latest satellite cloud pictures, to tell what kind of weather is in store for us.

Boats rely on regular wind forecasts. Gale warnings on the radio tell them the speed, direction and timing of approaching strong winds.

How strong is a strong wind?

Although weather maps show wind speed, what most people really want to know is what effects a strong wind will have. The Beaufort Scale does this, defining winds by what they do to their surroundings. Anything from force 10 up is officially a storm, but winds of forces 8 and 9 also cause a lot of damage.

The Beaufort Scale

Force 0: Calm. Smoke rises vertically.

Force 1: 1-5km/h (1-3mph) Light wind blows smoke.
Force 2: 6-11km/h (4-7mph) Light breeze.

Force 3: 12-19km/h (8-12mph) Leaves and twigs constantly move. Flags start to flutter.

Force 4: 20-29km/h (13-18mph) Moderate breeze. Dust and paper blown around. Small branches move.

Force 5: 30-39km/h (19-24mph) Fresh breeze. Small trees sway. Small waves on lakes.

Force 6: 40-50km/h (25-31mph) Strong breeze. Large branches on trees move. Difficult to use an umbrella.

Force 7: 51-61 km/h (32-38mph) Near gale force. Whole trees sway. Difficult to walk against the wind.

Force 8: 62-74km/h (39-46mph) Gale. Twigs broken off trees. Very difficult to walk.

Force 9: 75-87km/h (47-54mph) Severe gale. Damage to chimneys. Roof tiles blow off.

Force 10: 88-101km/h (55-63mph) Storm. Seldom occurs away from coasts. Trees uprooted. Buildings damaged.

Force 11: 102-117km/h (64-73mph) Violent storm. Very rarely occurs. Widespread damage.

Force 12: 118+km/h (74+mph) Hurricane. Total devastation.

Other scales describe specific storms in more detail. The Torro scale, forces T1-T12, classifies tornadoes by the damage they cause. A T12 supertornado can rip a whole house from its foundations and carry it away. Each hurricane area has its own grading system. Forces 1-5 describe hurricanes that hit the USA and the Philippines use a system of Public Storm Signals (PSS), forces 1-4.

Reading the clouds

Before sophisticated weather forecasting equipment was invented, clouds were the main way of predicting a storm. The key signs are still the same: cumulonumbus clouds thicken, the sky darkens, a wind starts and high level clouds speed across the sky. Today, the amount of cloud is measured on a scale of 0-8 oktas. 8 oktas means the sky is completely covered, 0 that it is clear.

An unusual cloud formation, called mamma, can be the signal for an approaching tornado or hailstorm.

Living with hurricanes

Hundreds of millions of people live in areas struck regularly by hurricanes, but many have never experienced a direct hit. Hospitals and schools hold "practices", so that everyone will know what to do when the real thing strikes.

Governments of risk areas publish safety booklets, but bad communications and education can make it hard to get vital information through. In some areas of Nepal, for example, less than half the population can read.

Waiting for the hurricane

As soon as a hurricane is spotted, a first alert, called a watch, is issued to all areas which may be in its path. When it is clear which area will be hit, urgent warnings are broadcast on radio and television.

Those in the path of a hurricane face a terrifying wait. People are advised to shelter above the highest predicted tide level, and to stock up on drinking water.

Escape is often difficult, as roads and bridges are quickly blocked by traffic, and may even be swept away as the winds arrive. Loose objects, including cars and trucks, need to be tied down, or risk being lost forever.

Why do people live there?

Often people have no choice. Hit by seven of the nine deadliest storms this century, Bangladesh is one of the poorest, most densely populated countries in the world.

There are 800 people per square km (2,000 per square mile). Many would rather risk frequent storms than live in the crowded city slums.

Walls of water

As the roaring winds approach, the first major hit of the hurricane, the storm surge, crashes down over the land. While still far out at sea, low pressure around the eye sucks water up into a great bulge.

Savage winds whip up smaller waves which spiral outward and are driven along in front of the hurricane. These can cover up to 1,500km (900 miles) a day, picking up more and more water until they crash against land as huge walls of water.

The worst, however, is yet to come, as the bulge of water around the eye is dumped in one colossal wave, often more than 3m (10ft) high. The biggest storm surges, which happen at high tide, can utterly destroy coastal towns and villages. In low-lying areas, flooding often follows.

The Bay of Biscayne lighthouse on Cape Florida before 1992's Hurricane Andrew ...

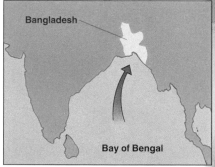
The Bay of Bengal is often hit by storm surges. Because it narrows sharply in the north, a surge of water will sweep away anything on the surrounding low land. There is nowhere to escape to.

Bangladesh

Bay of Bengal

Poisonous substances stream out of damaged factories, causing long-term damage to the environment.

Spilled oil can cause spectacular, but deadly, fires on the surface of the water.

Even water birds like ibis and heron cower in bushes to survive the killer winds, emerging to find only stumps to perch on.

Fish suffocate as fallen trees and plants eat up the oxygen in the water.

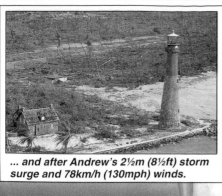
... and after Andrew's 2½m (8½ft) storm surge and 78km/h (130mph) winds.

Hurricanes often spawn tornadoes, which cause great local damage on land.

Flooding

As well as flooding from storm surges, hurricanes produce torrents of rain as the winds shed their moisture over mountains. In the Philippines in 1911, 116cm (46in) fell in one day. Very wet hurricanes are often the most powerful, as the condensation process is what gives a hurricane its energy.

The dragging force of flood water can cause huge damage. Walls crumble, windows splinter and floors sway like the deck of a ship before collapsing.

Rivers turn into torrents, with strong currents eating away at the foundations of houses or bridges, until they are simply swept away. Whole streets disappear as landslides pull the ground from underneath them.

Picking up the pieces

The complete cash crop of an area can be ruined in a few hours by winds that not only shake fruit from trees, but rip whole trees from the ground. Mango and coconut crops in Bangladesh are still recovering from their battering in horrific storms in 1991.

Famine often follows a severe hurricane. Bad storm surges contaminate valuable farmland with salt, which has to be drained off before the next crop can be grown.

Safe, dry buildings, called evacuation centers, are set up to feed and shelter the hungry and homeless. Many people lose everything they own. In very badly hit poorer areas, international aid programs are needed to restart farming and rebuild homes and businesses.

Whole orchards can be flattened by storm surges.

Did you know...

...that palm trees bend? And that some other plants, such as cycads, have been around longer than dinosaurs? Both have been forced to adapt to nature's wild ways and are tough enough to survive winds which would completely flatten non-tropical forests.

Cycad

Stray dogs and cats roam around, deserted as owners flee their homes.

Fast-moving water can overturn cars and turn floating debris into dangerous missiles.

Boats and small aircraft end up in unusual places, often mangled beyond repair.

Hurricane Hugo

Hurricane Hugo stormed through the Caribbean and into the USA in September 1989, causing the deaths of 82 people and $9 billion worth of damage.

Although not as costly as 1992's Hurricane Andrew (which cost around $30 billion), Hugo, at his peak a Force 4 hurricane, looms large in the minds of his battered victims. This page follows Hugo from his birth in Africa to his death halfway across the world.

Countdown to Hugo

Hurricane Hugo, like many Atlantic hurricanes, started off life as a West African depression, some 8,000km (5,625 miles) from where he eventually crashed onto land.

Within four days of the first sighting, the stormy depression boasted winds of over 117km/h (73mph). Now an official hurricane, the eighth of the 1989 season, he was given a name beginning with H, the eighth letter of the alphabet. Hugo had arrived.

Hurricane experts waited excitedly for satellite images to show how fast and how far the swirling cloud was advancing west.

This satellite image shows how Hugo began life as a mass of swirling cloud off the coast of West Africa.

A closer look

Two days later, air pressure in Hugo's eye plummeted to 918mb (27psi), way below the normal atmospheric pressure of 1013mb (29.9psi). Two aircraft set off for a closer look. One charged right into the hurricane to measure the winds, while the other cruised above the clouds, gathering radar images.

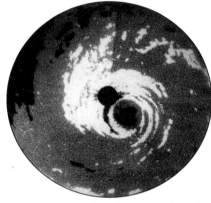

White curves in the middle of this radar image show the rain around Hugo's eye.

Air adventure

At 1.27pm on September 15, 1989, flight NOAA42 entered the cloud wall around Hugo's eye. The sky blackened, rain beat down and windspeed soared to 288km/h (180mph) in 90 seconds. For two whole minutes, the plane was tossed around by strong updrafts and downdrafts.

The pilot, on his 249th mission into a hurricane, managed to steer into the calm of the eye. Now only 200m (656ft) above lashing 20m (65ft) waves, there was only one way out. Would they make it back through the heaving cloud?

Forty-five nerve-wracking minutes later, an Air Force rescue plane arrived to guide the stricken plane through a thinner part of the eye wall. Flight NOAA42 took on Hugo's fury once again, to limp, shaken but safe, back to base.

Island hopping

At just over a week old, Hugo had his first stab at land. Thirty hours after the first warning, Guadeloupe's electricity shuddered to a halt. Homes were ruined and crops flattened as devastating winds swept through the island.

But Hugo carried on, relentlessly, to the northwest. Although only moving forward at around 13km/h (8mph), the winds kept up a steady 222km/h (138mph) roar, with gusts of up to 274km/h (164mph).

Radios around the Caribbean buzzed with warnings, advising the 161, 000 residents of Puerto Rico and the Virgin Islands to flee to safety shelters. As Hugo swept past, he threw down over 2,000mm (6½ ft) of rain, swelling many of Puerto Rico's steep rivers into dangerous torrents.

Hugo and the bat

The rare red fig-eating bat was almost wiped out forever, as Hugo swept through the Luquillo rain forest in Puerto Rico.

Bats play a vital role in helping forests recover from hurricanes, by scattering tree seeds. Luckily for Luquillo, a few of this rare species survived to rebuild the forest.

In some areas, whole forests were brought down by Hugo's fierce winds.

Hugo hits America

Two days later, Hugo bore down on mainland USA. Weather stations advised people in coastal areas to move - quickly. The town of Charleston in South Carolina had a 99% chance of being hit. Hugo's winds were expected to devastate an area 448km (280 miles) across, with tornadoes very likely.

By midnight on September 20, an endless stream of cars was heading to safety inland, with the remaining 216,000 residents ordered to flee the following morning.

Early on Friday, September 22 , South Carolina met Hugo. An enormous storm surge, in places 5m (17ft) above normal tide level, crashed down around Charleston.

Four hours later, the eye passed close to the inland city of Columbia. Another four hours farther inland, energy spent and winds weakening, Hugo was, at last, downgraded from hurricane to tropical storm.

The morning after

From a plane, cities that used to be a sea of light were indistinguishable from the black ocean. Two-thirds of eastern South Carolina was affected by power cuts, thousands of roofs had blown off, whole forests of trees had been uprooted, and killer mudslides had turned streets into swamps.

Where the colossal storm surge reached its peak, sturdy houses had completely disappeared and shrimp boats balanced awkwardly inland. Fields of pecan trees, corn and cotton lay flattened wastes.

Rain had damaged computers and other expensive electrical equipment inside buildings. South Carolina was not going to forget Hugo.

Roads were blocked by fallen trees, some slicing into cars or homes.

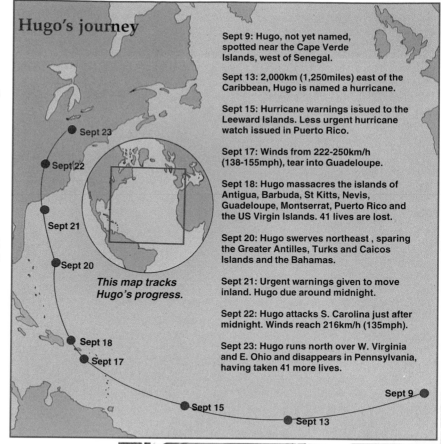

Hugo's journey

Sept 9: Hugo, not yet named, spotted near the Cape Verde Islands, west of Senegal.

Sept 13: 2,000km (1,250miles) east of the Caribbean, Hugo is named a hurricane.

Sept 15: Hurricane warnings issued to the Leeward Islands. Less urgent hurricane watch issued in Puerto Rico.

Sept 17: Winds from 222-250km/h (138-155mph), tear into Guadeloupe.

Sept 18: Hugo massacres the islands of Antigua, Barbuda, St Kitts, Nevis, Guadeloupe, Montserrat, Puerto Rico and the US Virgin Islands. 41 lives are lost.

Sept 20: Hugo swerves northeast , sparing the Greater Antilles, Turks and Caicos Islands and the Bahamas.

Sept 21: Urgent warnings given to move inland. Hugo due around midnight.

Sept 22: Hugo attacks S. Carolina just after midnight. Winds reach 216km/h (135mph).

Sept 23: Hugo runs north over W. Virginia and E. Ohio and disappears in Pennsylvania, having taken 41 more lives.

This map tracks Hugo's progress.

Sept 23
Sept 22
Sept 21
Sept 20
Sept 18
Sept 17
Sept 15
Sept 13
Sept 9

Floor after floor of windows were blown out and, in some buildings, whole walls were ripped away.

Destroyed stores were raided by hungry looters.

Hugo hitting land on September 22, 1989. Different shades on this satellite image show different temperatures. The deep, cold clouds around the eye show up clearly.

Shelter from the storm

Storm damage is generally at its most disastrous in areas which are not prepared for severe weather. Those living in the path of hurricanes know the dangers and have safety systems which swing into action when a warning is issued.

But, as global warming threatens to upset the balance of the world's storms (see page 28), more and more areas may find themselves regularly in the grip of dramatic and dangerous weather. Solid storm protection will be the key to saving lives.

Storm shelters

In low-lying coastal areas, mud and grass huts are no protection from hurricane winds and killer water. Specially built shelters are the most effective way of saving lives from ferocious gusts and 7m (23ft) high storm surges. In Bangladesh storms in 1991, all those who actually made it to a refuge survived.

Most shelters in Bangladesh are reinforced concrete boxes on one floor, raised about 6m (20ft) off the ground on concrete stilts. Some are large enough to shelter 2,000 to 3,000 people, with non-perishable food and drinking water stored inside.

Storm shelters along the Bangladesh coastline offer good storm protection and otherwise serve as schools or town halls.

Although more and more shelters are being built, they are costly and can only be erected in areas in real danger. Just one bag of cement is worth five days' pay in Bangladesh. It is hoped, however, that there will soon be enough shelters to protect two-thirds of the people living in high risk areas.

Tornado cellars

The best protection from tornadoes is underground. Many farms in Tornado Alley have specially reinforced cellars, called cyclone cellars, where people can shelter from approaching tornadoes.

The cellars have strong concrete walls and are around 1½ m (6ft) wide, 2½ m (8ft) long, and 2m (7ft) deep. This is big enough to hold at least 8 people. The door faces northeast, as most tornadoes come from the southwest, and has a strong bar inside it. This keeps it from flying open as the low pressure core of the tornado passes.

In houses with no cellar, the best place to shelter is in a closet or small room, in the middle of the house, away from windows.

Tornado or cyclone cellar

Heavy wooden door

Strong bar to keep door from flying open.

Building for strength

In many hurricane areas, there are codes which say how strong buildings should be. In parts of South Florida, USA, houses are built to withstand 192km/h (120mph) winds. Hospitals and schools need to protect the insides of their buildings as well. They can do this by installing backup power systems and bolting down all microscopes and other heavy machinery.

Not all homes live up to these standards. Mobile homes are particularly dangerous, but cannot be banned as they are the only homes many people can afford.

Cars are very unstable in storms. If you are in one as a tornado approaches, get out and lie in a ditch.

Storm shutters prevent wind from blowing in and deroofing houses from the inside.

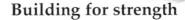

Storm shutters

Mobile homes are easily blown over.

Tall buildings

Tall buildings are especially risky in high winds, and many are reinforced with enormous steel frames, either inside or outside the walls.

The safest place to be in very strong winds, is on the ground floor, as near the middle of the building as possible.

The Bank of China in Hong Kong has steel cross-braces all the way up the outside to strengthen it.

Cross-bracing

Did you know...

...that many very tall buildings are actually designed to sway in high winds? This prevents the whole thing from toppling over. Some move more than lm (3ft) at the top, which can feel very odd to anybody inside.

Sydney Tower

Near the top of the Sydney Tower in Australia, there is a damping mechanism which helps to reduce the sway in high winds.

The damping mechanism consists of a heavy weight on a chain, attached to shock absorbers, like those in a car. It absorbs the energy of the wind.

Cold comfort

Hail and snowstorms cause havoc all over the world. Hail can ruin whole fields in minutes and farmers are always looking for new ways to protect their crops.

A freak snowstorm in a usually warm area can kill, through lack of protection as much as the cold itself. Many houses in Italy, for example, have no heating.

Hypothermia (a condition in which your body temperature falls dangerously low) is a serious risk when unexpectedly cold weather strikes.

Countries which suffer frequent snowstorms have building codes which specify a minimum depth of snow that roofs must be able to carry.

Italian farmers put matting roofs onto scaffold shelters to keep hail off their orange crops.

The wind flow pattern over roofs often causes snow to pile up dangerously heavily on one side.

Flood protection

Many cities on the coast have systems to keep out water from storm surges. Osaka, in Japan, has a series of arched barriers which can be lowered in just half an hour to protect the city from oncoming typhoons (hurricanes).

Even areas which do not at present suffer from hurricanes need protection from the seas. When a storm coincides with a very high tide in northern Europe, for example, storm surges can roll in and flood wide areas of land.

Holland has an extensive network of protective sea walls, called dykes, to protect its low-lying flat country. The Thames River, which flows through London, has a large barrier, consisting of ten huge gates which can be lowered if the sea level gets too high.

Along the coast in Japan, huge slabs of concrete are piled up to reinforce the shoreline and protect it from flooding.

Concrete slabs

This flat shore would flood very easily.

Earth's changing climate

The climate has been changing ever since the Earth began, from periods far warmer than today, where burning storms and volcanoes were common, to freezing ice ages. Many scientists think the Earth is getting warmer again and that this may increase the number of severe storms and hurricanes.

The global greenhouse

For millions of years, gases in the atmosphere have kept the Earth warm. These gases act like glass in a greenhouse, letting through the Sun's high energy heat waves but preventing heat radiated by the Earth from escaping. The Earth absorbs the trapped heat and stays at its present temperature. Without this so-called greenhouse effect, it would be too cold for us to survive.

Over the last couple of hundred years, however, there has been a build-up of carbon dioxide and other gases, often called "greenhouse" gases, in the atmosphere.

You can't see it and you can't smell it, but scientists believe that a thickening carbon dioxide blanket is gradually increasing temperatures all over the world. The amount of carbon dioxide could double by the year 2020, raising temperatures on Earth by 2-3°C (3.6-5.4°F).

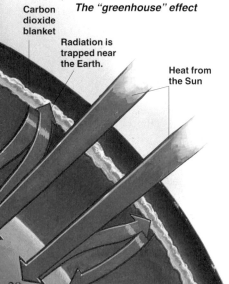

The "greenhouse" effect

Carbon dioxide blanket

Radiation is trapped near the Earth.

Heat from the Sun

Where "greenhouse" gases come from

Carbon dioxide and water vapor are the main gases which absorb outgoing radiation from the Earth, but there are others, including methane, nitrous oxides and chlorofluorocarbons (CFCs).

Carbon dioxide is given off by the burning of fossil fuels (coal and oil), mainly from power stations and factories.

Methane is given off from paddy fields, cattle and garbage. All three have increased with the world's soaring population.

The burning of forests and rotting vegetation add more carbon dioxide and methane to the atmosphere.

Chlorofluoro-carbons (CFCs) are given off by refrigerators and aerosol sprays.

Nitrous oxides come from exhaust fumes and fertilizers used on fields.

More storms?

By using computer models called general circulation models, or GCMs, weather experts can predict what effect global warming may have on our storms and hurricanes. It is thought that temperatures will rise unevenly over the globe, with cold polar areas changing most.

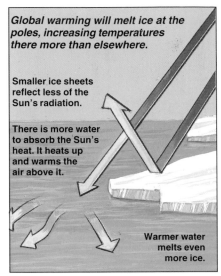

Global warming will melt ice at the poles, increasing temperatures there more than elsewhere.

Smaller ice sheets reflect less of the Sun's radiation.

There is more water to absorb the Sun's heat. It heats up and warms the air above it.

Warmer water melts even more ice.

Midlatitude storms (see page 6) are largely caused by depressions along the polar front. These develop because of a large difference in temperature between polar and tropical air masses.

If, as some experts believe, polar air gets warmer, this temperature difference will lessen, producing fewer deep depressions. This would mean fewer frontal storms.

More hurricanes?

Hurricanes, on the other hand, are expected to become more frequent. As tropical oceans warm up, more areas will have temperatures above the crucial 27°C (80°F) needed for hurricanes to form.

The increase in heat given off as more water vapor condenses may fuel the hurricanes into bigger, more fearsome machines than at present. Some tropical coasts could even become uninhabitable.

Warmer sea currents also mean that hurricanes will take longer to die out, putting greater stretches of coastal land at risk. It is thought that more may survive into mid-latitude as severe storm systems, or "ex-hurricanes", like the Great Storm in England in 1987. Mid-latitude areas may therefore see a decrease in medium-sized frontal storms (see left), but an increase in enormous hurricane-type ones.

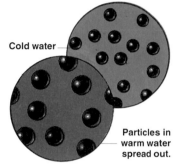

"Ex-hurricanes" may become frequent in western Europe.

Hurricane paths could stretch north along the highly populated USA east coast and the whole of Japan.

Even a small increase in sea temperatures would allow hurricanes to threaten the shores of Australia.

Rising sea levels

Over half the world's population lives within 50km (30 miles) of the sea. It is feared that global warming will cause sea levels to rise, making severe storm surges and bad flooding on low-lying coasts more likely. Experts think that sea levels could rise by as much as ½ m (1½ ft) over the next century.

Cold water

Particles in warm water spread out.

Like air, water expands when it is heated.

The 1,190 small coral islands which make up the Maldives in the Indian Ocean may disappear completely if sea levels rise.

One of the Maldives before (lower picture) and after (upper picture) a rise in sea levels.

Because water expands when it is heated, it occupies more space. But this is not the only reason for rising sea levels. As temperatures increase, the ice that permanently covers Antarctica will start to melt and flow into the sea. Frozen rivers, called glaciers, will add to the rising levels as they, too, melt and surge down mountains into the sea.

The result in countries like Bangladesh, where most of the land is only 5m (16ft) above sea level, would be catastrophic. Coasts would erode until much of the land simply disappeared underwater. Millions of people could lose their homes, and crops and fresh water reserves inland would be ruined by salt sea water.

Who is to blame?

Everyone is involved in what is happening to the planet. Wealthy industrialized countries are responsible for releasing 80% of "greenhouse" gases.

In developing countries, whole forests are cut down and burned to provide agricultural land. Huge amounts of carbon dioxide, locked up for years as carbon in tree trunks, is released all at once back into the atmosphere as the trees burn. Despite wide replanting schemes, much more forest is destroyed each year than is replaced.

Experiments have been carried out to look at ways of reducing carbon dioxide levels, but so far, no practical solution has been found.

This woman in Bangladesh is pumping fresh water from a pump that has been completely cut off by salty flood water.

Floods have already claimed much valuable farmland in Bangladesh. Rising sea levels will only make the problem worse.

Storms on other planets

When you are caught in a particularly bad storm, it can be difficult to imagine how the weather could ever get any more ferocious. But even the fiercest storms on Earth are small fry compared to storms on some of the other planets.

Cold storms

Streams of freezing wispy cloud, and storms shaped like ovals, race around the planet Neptune, driven by some of the strongest winds in the Solar System. From bands of darker clouds, one particularly large storm stands out. Called the Great Dark Spot, this icy storm is 8km (5 miles) wide, 12km (7.4 miles) long) and rages continuously.

Neptune

The Great Dark Spot

The Great Red Spot

The Great Red Spot, on the surface of the planet Jupiter, is a giant of a storm. Around 8km (5 miles) high, 40,000km (25,000 miles) long and 14,000km (8,700 miles) wide, it has been blowing for about 300 years.

Jupiter's atmosphere is made up of layers of swirling gases. Very high winds break up the icy cloud tops of the outer layer into streams of red, brown, orange and yellow clouds. Beneath the clouds are turbulent layers of hotter gases. The Great Red Spot is powered by these hot gases surging up from Jupiter's bubbling depths.

Jupiter

The Great Red Spot

The spinning winds of the Great Red Spot reach 500km/h (310mph). This is stronger than the strongest winds in a tornado on Earth.

Sun

Venus

Space greenhouse

The surface temperature on Venus, second closest planet to the Sun, is around 482°C (900°F) - hot enough to melt lead and twice as hot as the hottest kitchen oven. This is largely because Venus has a runaway greenhouse effect, with an atmosphere of about 98% carbon dioxide.

The Sun's heat is trapped between 50 and 75km (30 and 45 miles) above the surface of the planet. It is feared that the Earth may go the same way as Venus if we keep adding carbon dioxide to the atmosphere.

Storms on Venus produce burning sulphuric acid rain, which means nothing could live there. Acid rain occurs on Earth too, as toxic factory waste mixes with water vapor and condenses into cloud droplets of sulphuric or nitric acid. Acid rain can kill whole forests and even dissolve rocks.

Dust storm on Mars

The atmosphere around Mars is very thin, which means that there are hardly any gases and virtually no water vapor in it. This leaves Mars a very cold and dry planet, with high winds and frequent dust storms.

In 1971, a dust storm covered the whole of the planet. Clouds of dust trapped in large craters showed up as white spots on space probe photographs.

Crater

Glossary

Air mass. A large quantity of air that has the same level of humidity and temperature throughout.

Anemometer. An instrument used for measuring the speed of the **wind**.

Atmospheric pressure (air pressure). The weight of air pushing down on a unit area of a planet's surface.

Barometer. An instrument used for measuring **air pressure**.

Beaufort Scale. A scale used for measuring the strength of the **wind**, based on observations.

Blizzard. A storm of powdery snow or ice carried by **gale** force **winds**, during which visibility is poor.

Coalescence. The process by which water droplets in a cloud collide and come together to form raindrops.

Cloud seeding. An experimental process used to weaken **hurricanes** or "rainmake" in dry areas.

Cold front. The boundary between a cold **air mass** and a warm **air mass**, where the cold air moves in to replace the warmer air.

Condensation. The process by which a gas or vapor changes into a liquid.

Conductor. Any substance or object which carries (conducts) electricity.

Convection. The upward movement of air which has been heated by the land or sea surface below.

Coriolis effect. The effect caused by the Earth's rotation which deflects air moving between two places.

Cumulonimbus clouds. Towering storm clouds, associated with heavy rain, **thunder** and **tornadoes**.

Cyclone (also called a **depression**). An area of low pressure, often causing unsettled weather.

Depression (see **cyclone**).

Dew point. The temperature at which water vapor in the air condenses to form water.

Dust devil. A tight **whirlwind** which picks up dust as it spins.

Dust storm. Strong **winds** which whip up and blow dust into huge dust clouds.

Evaporation. A process by which a liquid changes into a gas or vapor.

Eye. The central column of slowly sinking air in a **hurricane**, where **winds** are light and the air is warm.

Front. The boundary that separates two **air masses** with different temperatures.

Gale. A **wind** with an average speed of over 62km/h (39mph). Force 8 on the **Beaufort Scale**.

Geostationary satellite. A weather satellite which hovers 36,000km (22,370miles) above one place on the Earth's surface.

Global warming. An overall increase in world temperatures which may be caused by additional heat being trapped by **greenhouse** gases.

Greenhouse effect. The heating effect caused by gases in the atmosphere, mainly carbon dioxide, trapping heat (radiation) from escaping into space.

Humidity. The amount of water vapor in the air.

Hurricane (also called **typhoon** or **willy-willy**). A severe storm, with torrential rain, strong **winds** and a calm **eye**, formed over warm seas between 5° and 20° N and S of the Equator.

Hygrometer. An instrument which measures the **humidity** of the air.

Intertropical Convergence Zone (ITCZ). A band of low pressure around the Equator, where warm air rises and is replaced by air moving in from the northern and southern hemispheres.

Isobar. A line on a weather map joining places with the same **atmospheric pressure**.

Jet stream. Fast currents of high-level **wind** which circle the Earth 10-16km (6 -10 miles) above the surface.

Lightning. Static electricity discharged as a flash from **cumulonimbus clouds**.

Magnetosphere. The boundary between the Earth's atmosphere and space.

Microburst. A strong current of air which shoots down through a **cumulonimbus cloud** and produces heavy rain.

Mid-latitude areas. Areas between 30° and 60° N and S of the Equator.

Monsoon. A **wind** which blows from opposite directions at different times of the year, creating a rainy and a dry season.

Occluded front. A front which occurs where a **cold front** undercuts a **warm front**, lifting warm air from the surface.

Ozone layer. A layer of ozone gas, found in the **stratosphere**, which absorbs harmful radiation from the Sun.

Polar front. Where the leading edge of cool polar air meets warmer air.

Polar orbiting satellite. A weather satellite which travels over both poles each time it orbits the Earth, 850km (530 miles) high.

Stratosphere. The smooth layer of the Earth's atmosphere where temperature does not decrease with height. Contains the **ozone layer**.

Storm surge. A huge wave, or series of waves, which break over land, caused by water sucked up into the low pressure center of an approaching storm.

Thermal. A rising current of warm air caused by a local area of the Earth's surface heating up more than its surroundings.

Thunder. The noise caused by the rapid expansion of air in a stroke of **lightning**.

Tornado. A violent **whirlwind** which descends from a **cumulonimbus cloud**, with an extremely low pressure core.

Tropical areas. Areas of the Earth within 20°N and S of the Equator.

Tropical cyclone. Collective name for a **hurricane**, **typhoon** or **willy-willy**.

Troposphere. The turbulent bottom layer of the Earth's atmosphere, where all our weather takes place.

Warm front. The boundary between a warm **air mass** and a cold **air mass**, where the warm air moves in to replace the cooler air.

Waterspout. A **whirlwind** which descends from a **cumulonimbus cloud** and sucks up water as it touches the sea.

Whirlwind. A small, rotating storm, where air whirls around a core of low pressure.

Wind. The movement of air between high pressure and lower pressure areas.

Wind funnel. Strong **wind** that blows down a valley, or through a narrow gap.

Index

Picture credits

Page 4: cyclone damage, Bangladesh © B. Klass/Panos Pictures
Page 8: Bangledesh floods © Trygve Bølstad/ Panos Pictures
Page 10: lightning © 1995, Comstock Inc.
Page 12: polarised light photo of giant hailstone © NCAR/Science Photo Library
Page 15: waterspout © J.G.Golden/ Science Photo Library
Page 15: dust devil © Warren Faidley/ Oxford Scientific Films
Page 16: computer-generated image of Hurricane Allen © Hasler & Pierce, NASA GSFC/Science Photo Library
Page 18: infrared satellite images of Hurricane Gilbert/Courtesy NOAA
Page 18: visible satellite image/Courtesy NASA Goddard Space Flight Center
Page 19: radar image of Hurricane Allen/ Courtesy NOAA
Page 21: mamma clouds © J.Schahinger
Pages 22, 23: Cape Florida lighthouse, before and after Hurricane Andrew © 1995 Comstock Inc.
Page 24: satellite image of Hurricane Hugo/ Courtesy NOAA
Page 24: radar image of Hurricane Hugo/ Courtesy NASA
Page 25: false-color satellite image of Hurricane Hugo © Dr Fred Espenak/ Science Photo Library.
Page 26: cyclone shelter © Zed Nelson/ Panos Pictures
Page 29: rising flood water © Jim Holmes/ Panos Pictures

The publishers are grateful to the following people and organizations for provision of information and/or materials for use as artists' reference:

Dr. Roger D Trend, National Climatic Data Center, American Meteorological Society, Asian Disaster Preparedness Center, Tony Fitzpatrick of Ove Arup and Partners, Royal Meteorological Society, Rutherford Appleton Laboratory, National Meteorological Library

Copyright © 1995 by Usborne Publishing Ltd. All rights reserved. Published by Scholastic Inc., 555 Broadway, New York, NY 10012, by arrangement with Usborne Publishing Ltd.

12 11 10 9 8 7 6 5 4 3   6 7 8 9/9 0 1/0

Printed in the U.S.A.   09

First Scholastic printing, September 1996